Bubble Gum
at the
Register

Bubble Gum at the Register

POEMS

MARY MANHATTAN

ILLUMIFY
MEDIA.COM

Copyright © 2023 Mary Manhattan

Published by
Illumify Media Global
www.IllumifyMedia.com
"Let's bring your book to life!"

Paperback ISBN: 978-1-959099-61-1

Typeset by Art Innovations (http://artinnovations.in/)
Cover design by Curry Mendes Artist (https://currymendes.com/)

Printed in the United States of America

To the love of my life, my husband, for his
eternal optimism, inspiration, and his love

contents

acknowledgements

This book would not be possible without my husband's help and encouragement. I am most grateful to my editors—Bob, Mom, Dad, Charlie, Ginny, Connie and Frank, Dr. Clemente—for their suggestions, honesty, and laughter. Many thanks go to my brother, sisters, and brothers-in-law, for help with the title and introduction. The team at Illumify Media has been wonderful and I am thankful for their assistance.

And, of course, I am truly appreciative of all of those circumstances and people that pushed me to the brink of insanity. Survival is excellent motivation. I'm back…

preface

Love is war! Nah, it really isn't. Though if you do choose to battle, the fields of play are sex and money for that fleeting, wistful illusion of control. What you are about to read is a love story and life story. It is chock-full of poetic license, not quite a biography, but a bit of a journal dashed off in the heat of the moment.

I am not, nor have I ever been, suicidal. Any resemblance to real persons living or dead, or actual events, places, buildings, and products is purely coincidental. Identification with same is not intended and should not be inferred. It is, after all, entirely possible that I've met a few unprincipled, gaslighting, narcissists over the years, and a lawsuit by you is just you outing you. Get over yourself, bucko. No animals were harmed in the making of this book.

—Mary Manhattan
New York, 2023

foreword

Why choose a book of poems over other forms of storytelling? Mary Manhattan answers this question beautifully through her writing. She captivates us with a series of skillfully crafted poems that spark our imagination and leave a lasting impact.

Upon reading the initial poems in this collection, I was transported back to my college freshman year, where poetry held a deeper significance beyond the beautiful verses of high school. *Bubble Gum at the Register* is undeniably thought-provoking, offering a range of experiences. While not every poem demands deep contemplation, some possess a poetic charm that resonates with our senses, past, and current circumstances.

Throughout my reading, I often paused to appreciate the unique phrasing and skillful arrangement of words that wove captivating narratives. The author's emotions are palpable—whether it's hope, anxiety, or amusement.

Let me spotlight three particular poems. "Doubts" conveys both anguish and hope, striking a chord across generations entangled in our intricate world.

In just fourteen words, "Lack of view" conveys a crucial lesson that everyone could use a reminder of.

"What can be done with this piece of paper" exudes whimsy while imparting a lesson on the boundless potential of ordinary objects. It nudges us to embrace our imagination more fervently.

Certainly, each reader will uncover their personal favorites. My challenge for you is to narrow down to three, a task that's daunting due to the abundance of depth within these pages.

This poetry collection is bound to become a perennial reread, promising years of enrichment.

—Edward R. Del Gaizo
Author of several books, including:
Rose's Gamble: A biographical account of one woman's determination for a better life for her family

The Goal

gracefully gliding
rapid water ready to
rise above the ridge

    raging rivers breach
    the banks and then recede to
    subtle flows at last

river banks so safe
restricting guiding streams to
sea your only goal

Handbag

Big Soft
Carrying a world
I KNOW it's in here
Comfort

Owned

My cat rubs and marks
me as if to say Now you
are mine! I agree.

Helper

Dissatisfied not
disillusioned, I look out
for my neighbor's dog.

Vision

I had a vision
    crisp clear bright.
I pulled the shade
    lest I die of fright.

Diner

You have
your choice of eats.
Hamburger. Chile. Soup.
What'll you have mister, that'll
fill you
up.

Circumstances

A good martyr
    I would not make
You force me you force
me I try Warning!
    Warning!

As a martyr
    I will not last
You want peace you want
peace I sigh Warning.
    Warning!

A hefty price
    I do pay
You too pay you do
pay I try Warning.
    Warning.

I choose my price.
I pay you pay I
pray.

The Hollow

Dark cavernous damp and hollow
   ...your mind
    is a frightful place.

I sneak a peek when you scream
   ...vast and cold...

I took   a look   and knew

      a soul
was lost   in there.

sore spot - nut shot

HEY! I didn't know I had these balls!
Though now that we've met... I see... I do.
So now, each day i coat 'em in titanium
to keep 'em safe – from you!

Other Plans

This week was shot to hell,
wasting time on you.
Don't blow my weekend now.
I've got better things to do.

A Call to Arms

In this war...
expose my worst,
and I will bring out my best.

I'll do the
same for you.

You say   I say

you say you love me   I say I love you
I believe   I believe
you believe   you believe
it's true   it's true

                    but I believe
                      it's false

First Love

I gave my heart,
and it was not cared for.
I got no heart in return
and took no notice.

Bleeding hearts need stiches of love;
the sooner given – the better healed.
Hearts mend and scar.

Doubts

In the corner of my mind
    is a doubt
gnawing away at my brain.
Am I the one that's not living
    in reality,
    or is it the world
  that is insane?
I might just have a touch of paranoia,
but I think justifiably so.
In this life that I am in,
    I feel,
    I have no place to go.
But I will continue,
  to search for the truth,
  to satisfy the curiosity,
  and wipe away all doubt.
I am sure I will find out what
    is up,
    what is down,
  and who may know
if they're still around.

Youth

No, don't tell me you're not young anymore.
What is age
but the price you pay for knowledge?
    I'd rather you tell me
    you can't love me
    for my insecurities
    that age hasn't worked away,
    for my brutal honesty
    that age hasn't softened,
    or for my inexperience
    that my age cannot attain.

Emphasis: Free

I can
remember my
first love and what made it
so special. I gave
everything
free.

Look up

On my way in –
finally, relief from the wind.
I pass them as I wipe wet feet on gray carpet.
They stare – each one – all   three   stare.
I check my nose; no, not dripping.

The guard glances
          stares   well
                         below
          my smile.

Fool   look   outside.
If only you could properly read the signs –
not an invitation,
my front, just a weather report.
It's cold!

Yup

By God, I'm getting out of this hole
I dug for myself.
And when I do that
I'll build myself a shelf.

The Other Art - Sunnie Suzie

When thin appear fat
Blousy shirts and flowing skirts
Attract attention
        ~ Sunnie Suzie

Whatever you've got
Push 'em up and together
Ensures unity
        ~ Sunnie Suzie

The Other Art - Sunnie Suzie

When fat appear thin
Vertical stripes in dark hues
Sunny skies ensue
     ~ Sunnie Suzie

Cooperation
In creation ~ merciful
hopeful heritage
     ~ Sunnie Suzie

First date - *Cosmo* style

Firstly, shower off daily living. Pat body dry.
  Do not rub.
Apply lotion liberally for silky smooth skin.
Rub a dab of
the indispensable gel for well-groomed hair
between palms and fingers.
  Shape hair. Dry naturally. Style as usual.
Glide on the specially designed fresh scent
  for women
that will plug pores, prevent nervous
  perspiration, protect clothes
  and dignity.
(As the Indian warrior would prepare to
  protect his territory, I will paint my face
  to conquer.)
Lastly, arrange hand towels. Hide
  tampons, birth control.
Softly pitter patter down the hall.
  Double check face, posture
  in mirror. Answer bell.

82nd

Fatigues then fatigued
TO FLIGHT ALL AMERICAN
Summer thanks in waves

Rivals

rivals slavishly
riveted to passion in
bloom both now servile

Envy

envy dripping down
puddling around ... sticky
holding you there fast

Distraction

now i scream so quietly that
you have to turn up the TV
to muffle my silence

2 4 6 5 3 1

so rare
inspiration
when it comes through my soul
cries out justice now
inspire
me

Persist

Today's attempt was not that good.
Tomorrow's could be better.
The day after that would improve,
if pride would only let her.

Fearful dreaming Haiku

I fear you are a
dream! Praise God! Dreams come complete
with senses intact.

If the fear be real,
I pray continual rest –
this vision shall live!

Succession

You ceded the ground you clearly had won,
Salted that mountain thinking all was done.
Made him a father, moved on, walked away.
You exuded confidence that exceedingly quiet day.

Scoping out the field of battle,
I set my steps, so far unrattled.
Preparing for the rocky climb,
Flying under radar, for a time.

The loot, the spoils, and the like
    do take time to get just right.
Surveys of sky, land, and sea
    help determine the best L.Z.

It's a war zone I entered, or so I thought.
A pause in action after you two had fought.
A trap, a ruse, fire fights await!
You must be lurking. Was this some unknown bait?

What kind of fool would walk away from this prize?
How could you choose to lose one so strong, true, and wise?

I admit it took me a bit to see
You saw yourself basking in everlasting victory.
"Hilarious," I thought, "you're such an elf."
I pay no mind to what you thought of yourself.

I braced for impact, as I looked around.
"Good to see you," you said. At last, I was found.
No peace, nor treaty. The outcome was sealed.
"Good to be seen!" said I, scanning the field.

I was born for this, which had you completely incensed.
Risks were calculated and combat commenced.
Hold tight, my friend, a life of love is worth the cost.
Stay close, my friend. Until Valhalla! All is not lost!

Normalcy

Living, by any standard, a
    somewhat
    normal life,
filled with a
    somewhat,
    normal experiences
walking a
    somewhat
    straight path
on a
    somewhat
    sane Earth,
is not living

It is merely existing,
with eyes closed.

Because this earth is
filled with
insanity. And by
    standards taught,
    the norm,
is actually not.

It might take more
than you thought
to live in this world,
    on this earth,
but someone had to be
    born here.

May John Donne Forgive Me

Layoff, be not proud, though some have called thee
Rightsizing, for thou art not so;
For those whom though think'st thou dost unemploy
Leisure not, poor Layoff, nor yet canst thou unemploy me,
From "right" and "down" which but thy sizes be,
Much laughter; then from thee improved returns must flow,
And soonest our best with thee do go,
Skills sown through tenure here and others reap.
Thou art slave to consultants and desperate men,
And dost with budgets and rivalry dwell,
And motivation can improve it as well!
And better than thy stroke; why swell'st thou then?
One short layoff past, work 'til retiring,
And Layoff shall be no more; Layoff thou dost lie.

Lack of view

nickels and dimes will
get you a cup of coffee
not a mountain view

Money sounds

money crinkles like
autumn leaves and listens for
sounds of destruction

Money speaks

If money could speak, would it scream
   "Don't waste time making me!
   Make time!
   Make your wife!"
then continue softly
"I take time, your life... take me!"

Just Desserts

**(Or, "every dog has its day," or "you reap what you sow,"
or "what goes around, comes around."
But mostly, "payback is a bitch.")**

When the time comes,
when payback knocks,
will you know who she is?
Will you open the door?

Doesn't matter. She'll POUND!!
She was sent to do a job and she *will* do it.

Regardless of whether or not or if or when
you get the message.

Special-delivery-custom-designed-made-to-order
    second chance.

Adoring flowers

You? Child.
Page. Slender serving. Blossom.

Him? Father.
Book. Immense banquet. Bouquet.

Inheritance

You were meant to inherit
    Forgiveness that breeds
        Faith to fill you with
            Hope that'll eventually bring
        Charity that puts you in a mind for
    Forgiveness.
Spiraling – forever – spiraling.

      You chose to take
      Greed that bred
    Envy to fill you with
Hate that eventually brought
    Covetousness that put you in a mind for
      Greed,
      Spiraling   still.

Ohhh! You thought I was supposed
to continually bestow these on you! How funny!

No. You were supposed
to take them, make them your own
    so your children could
      Inherit something good
    so you'd have something good for your
children to inherit.

Fortunately, due to the nature of the inheritance,
I can continually bestow these on you.

    Now, let me enjoy your children's inheritance.

Madam to Maiden

His lips are roses over-washed with dew...
     And stew.
Well, his eyes are bright and calm as the serenest noon
and the gleam is pearly...
     His moon eyes never opened that early.
Still, his face in a certain slant of light brings to mind an
April morn...
     Muddy and torn.
His arms caress as if opened by heaven's light!
     Heaven? That's on Forty-Second and Eighth, right?
A thing of beauty to behold and oh, so clever...
     Acckkk! A ball and chain forever.

Gruesome

You were so gruesome today.
Being gruff got you your way.
Grumbling the grumpiest grunt,
you staged the stupidest stunt.
So I've been asked to relay
this short communique,
"every dog has its day, you runt!"
> *(I did say the 'r' word, didn't I?*
> *I coo that call the time... tee hee.)*

Prophet

Were you,
Nostradamus,
a man who saw through time?
Or just sufficiently vague to
interest
still?

Dancing with Air

Truth is not determined by democratic vote,
despite your being American and so, so
determined to convince and believe such and such,
the truth just is. Regardless of the pains you'll go;
insisting doesn't make it so.

Chatter and whispers hurt and hurtful looks haunted
for a while. No more. I was there and I know.
Unlike your legions, ready to believe your sad
tale, half unspoken, told through sighs and pouts, your tears
injecting half-truths into fears.

The mastery with which you manipulate the
crowd is nothing short of artistic bullying.
And shame on them for buying it! Unquestioning
silence encourages the deception. As yet,
they believe the lie you forget.

So quick to fight and judge; fear rules you.
You know I know how low you will go.
I strongly suggest you sow some seeds
of truth before you are forced to reap.

No threat implied and no threat intended. Cosmic
justice will deal with you. I have written you off.
Karma slams you now, and you don't even know what
hit you. It's aura-add-on! Image enhancer!
Victim's soul — the shadow dancer.

Confronted with your perceptions, you cry, deny,
yell, say "I'm sorry"; then twist up some new lies so
that I'd apologize! It takes two to tango.
I've stopped dancing. Your soiled soul so unaware
I watch you there dancing with air.

Despite your campaign compelling crowds to believe,
your deliberate attempts to connive and deceive,
truth is not determined by democratic vote.

You are on your own.

Vapor

At times my fury
makes me cry. I weep so hard, laughing.
You should too.

Please tell me how my words hurt you.
These puny   puffs of air put   out   there...
Thoughts turned into sound by chords and breath.
These   frustration vents (-- puff--)
    (-- pouf--)
Evaporating.

Opportunity!
From just one outburst, you could learn
what a year's worth
of polite conversation would earn.

man up

I don't
want to jump down
your throat. I don't want to
be told I'm silly
but to be
shown.

Without a paddle

(5-7-5+ season/time passing/nature - what'd I miss?)

up to the neck in
shit more shit deep smelly shit ~
learn to swim this fall

'Tis the Marching Season

'Tis the marching season.
March on orange   proud   drums   march.
            I smile yet won't be at your parade.
But, fly your flag. I know.

'Tis the marching season.
March on colors   loud   victor   march.
            No, I won't be at your parade.

I smile at your reason for your marching season,
trading a pope for a king.
March on orange   proud   drums   march.
Argue infallibility with me, then
March on colors   loud   victor   march.

One   two   three   hundred years ago, now
your king conquered and so
'Tis your marching season
and on you go.
            Is that all?

One   two   *thousand*   years   ago, or so,
a carpenter conquered death.
I thank Him with each and every breath.
And on I go.
            That   *is*   *all*.

March on flags fly drums   pound victor.
I know.

'Tis the marching season.
No, I won't be at your parade.

Victim's Villain

What lies ahead is not for the meek,
nor was that which formed it.
Fever broken, not content to sit,
the victim's villain will speak.

Verdict

The jury knotted will wait.
The Judge and victims still ache.
As justice sits sidelined.
The villain-vulture unwinds.

ppppp

poetry
    pointing out
        poisons
    permeating
people

words sounds

(6 months' difference)

October.
Something some Nazi might scream to his comrade.
Crisp,
it cuts the cold clear night.

April.
Something some lassie might sing to her lapdog.
Light,
it lifts the lazy morn.

Therapy

She walks silently
    to the room
with the plastic chairs
and (fake) wooden tables
    each week.

Therapy.

The delicate art
    of
instilling the will to live.

She had screamed and slashed,
slashed and screamed,
hoping (for the first time in all her 15 years)
    ...really all she wanted to do
was finish the job they had started.

Drain the blood from her body
    via two wrists.

Because her life was gone anyway.
It had been pressed so long it squeezed out.

Every day, every long night she saw it ooze
    out
    with her sweat.

A lot

Sex sometimes reminds us to be hopeful,
we may yet leave a legacy on earth.
Those delicious acts could result in birth
and life and duty; quick decisions pull
and push and mold; relentless work; to cull
goodness, kindness and so define one's worth.
The world in one small child, full of mirth
and joy, ready to learn and teach; you're full!
I'm not, can't, so don't. Blest, yet put to test.
While others without much thought, most with fear
and no clear choosing, bring life in or not.
No options, nor empathy. It is best
to honor thy father and mother here
as their legacy; this life is our lot.

Resumé

(with apologies to Dorothy Parker)

Fishing bores you;
Naps are no answer;
Golfing poors you;
And tans cause cancer.

Drugs aren't lawful;
Kids cry and jerk;
School is awful;
You might as well work!

Hippocrene

Hippocrene, Hippocrene, flow to my mind.
Hippocrene currents flow throughout time.
Inspiration font pours on people.
Hippocrene muses now on the steeple.

Steeple high and
steeple tall,
from you I see the beauty in all.

Steeple sharp and
steeple long,
your walls tell stories of days bygone.

Steeple sturdy,
steeple strong,
through time you truly see what went wrong

Steeple old and
steeple wise,
show me wisdom through your windowed eyes.

Hippocrene, Hippocrene flows through ages.
Hippocrene drops across my pages.
Hurry, amuse me though it's so late.
Hippocrene, Hippocrene, of course, I'll wait!

1234

1	2
MUSIC ON	MUSIC ON
SONG PLAY	LISTEN GOOD
LISA GONE	LISA GONE
ONE DAY	SHE SHOULD

3	4
MUSIC ON	MUSIC OFF
OFF SOON	MUSIC GONE
LISA GONE	LISA SING
FULL MOON	A SONG

Poetry

Poetry ~
like a sweet song
sung by a humming bird
when Old Man Winter has finally given
            up the fight.
It's warm again.
Missed,
like May flowers and April showers.
Poetry ~
quietly caressing your mind.
It sweeps you up from behind
like the warm winds of summer
carrying an old leaf left over from fall.
Poetry ~
always there to open your heart
like the first time in spring
you take down the storm windows
to let fresh, warm air into your home.

Muse

Oh, the pens and papers I could use
if only I were inspired by my muse.
Has she forgotten me?

Airborne!

All American
All the way ~ march, glide & slide
Bring it home today

Sex

Sex like sunrise is
the best part of a day and
inspires success.

Sign in. Sign out.

Sign in.
Sign out.
It doesn't matter why,
just do what I say
and you'll be ok
and I'm sure you'll get by.
Are you here?
Are you there?
Are you where you should be?
Just do what I say
and you'll be ok,
it really doesn't matter if you see.
Did you leave?
You shouldn't have, you know.
Just do what I say
and you'll be ok.
"No, I can't let you go.
I don't make the rules.
They come with the schools."
I just
don't
buy it.

My Center

Gravity? orbit's
pull? My path is steadied by
your force; gentle, kind.

Economy of Words

I hear, "Hey, wife!"
    and I know who is called
    and who is calling!
Precisely. Quite an economy of words.

I call on my Muse
    and you know who I am
    and who I want
    and by who I am calling, why!

One God, many names
    (not blasphemy nor untruth).
    I enhance my prayer
    through economy of words.

imperfect haiku

Lizzie BB's depths
"Translations from Esquanish."
Does Basho forgive?

Unmoved Immortality

Tenderly Judged by History
Dismissed by poet peers
Undaunted – you heard and shared your Voice
It rings true – after all these years

Gentlest heart – softest soul
Steadfastly singing on
In your time – known to just a few
Now kindly looked upon

I measure your melodies
Most familiar and dear –
I pleasure in their meaning
Though they mayn't be that Clear

Is there – then – a pair of us?
I doubt that could be so
You have no match – unmoved – no mate
Eternal voice endures – alone

I find Hope in every Poem –
Lines Light and Glorious as dew
Truly now – I imagine
Your peers found that – in you

Surely – a different drum stroke
echoed only for you
While – sweet soul – armed only with ink
Wondered on the World – still – marched on

Your soul selected a Society
Larger than the few you knew
Or – Emily – I think it much more True
Society's Soul Selected You

Reconcile

Every hour of every day
God provides in every way.

Every minute of every hour
God provides us with the power.

Every second of every minute
God provides, for He is in it.

Every moment in every life,
God provides, yet we provide strife.

Well-Seasoned Senses

the aluminum
door held tight to wet finger-
tips, aided by cold

tender shoots peek out
of our earth as if proving
spring really is here

barbecue scents hang
heavy in hot humid air
inviting neighbors

crinkling crackling leaves
scoot quietly across the
street   still   I hear them

harvest and gather
our dreams! truly ...each bite tastes
better than the last

well-seasoned senses
know the earth moon stars call love
to you all for you

I felt the shift

He and I are slipping
Sliding slowly apart
I think that's the worst way
It's hardest on the heart

Fidelity

Forty seasons brought
us strength, hope, faith, charity,
no illusions, love.

Reveal it again

In an instant
I see it all fall into place.
And in that instant
I can't find the words.

In an instant
I see it all fall away.
What bits and pieces remain
Leave me more confused than ever.

Whistle in the Dark

The train is riding passed our town,
moving with that steady humming sound.
    Slowly singing me to sleep,
    convincing me not to weep.
The whistle blows
    while the night-time goes,
away with the trains.

Pirouette

my mind dances on an empty page
    too   too
        many   thoughts emotions   worlds
to tuck neatly   into   tiny   little   words.

but dance I do,   we do
fill the page,
      pages
        and more.

my soul dances
      gliding   slipping.
      I   try to tie this thought
to that word
      this world to that thought   emotion.

another page
      full   volumes
      ...turn...
another empty page

to dance the dance again

The search

Freedom
   is the most cherished
   gift I have.
  As goes human nature,
   I did not realize this
   great love for
Freedom
   until I no longer had
   as much as before.
  So now –
Freedom
   is what I am,
   vigorously,
   searching for.

Performance Review

Look closely
at him acting all,
"I'll help you!"

Look closer.
Changed his mind again,
didn't he...

See it yet?
He's a captured pawn.
You are sovereign.

What color will our revolution be?

Fall Fail

The leaves sound dry
            I say
             burn
        on   up

Growing into Change

Guess the frying pan looks good right about now.
When will you stop adding fuel to the fire, and how?
What will it take for you to finally see?
You've got to change, not me.

You never thought things could get this bad.
It'd make a good movie or book, however sad.
The hardest part is to see innocence squirm.
You've got to change, when will you learn?

Waking

People just waking, and the sun
     is bright.
It's morning now but I'm not afraid of
     the light.
You're still holding me near
     and calling me dear,
     and I love you.

Silent Creation

Snow ~ fluffy blankets ~
God's creation covering
earth in quiet. Shhhh!

In the beginning was the Word

The power of a word
to evoke a feeling, solve a mystery,
so amazes me. Each word
is chosen so carefully.

God, the Artist

Petals,
God's confetti,
dotting manicured lawns.
Jackson Pollock could not compete!
Messy Magnolia vomits
over man's design.
I smile.
Art.

2 4 6 5 3 1 . 2

Didja'
ever meet a
chick who thought love could be
bought by giving birth?
I did; I
ran.

Direct Access Remote Control

(DARC)

Now
More than 600 worlds may pass through my living room
With one finger

March 1, 1988

If I gather bunches of words
and place them in a basket,
will you arrange them
into a pleasing bouquet?

Safe

The fire burned itself out.
A soft whisper surrounds you,
encases you. God is here.

It began

So it started with
a song, sonnet or haiku
these poems flow to you.

What can be done with this piece of paper

Fold it, mold it, make it cold, but keep your hold.
Will it be sold? No. It's too old.
Put it on the wall, in the hall, roll it in a ball,
and all.
Rip it up, stash it in a cup.
Write on it, bite on it, hold tight on it.
Throw it out.
Leave it, heave it.
Keep it, sleep on it.
Read it, heed it.
Put it in your pocket, hock it.
Hang it, bang it.
Put it on fire, hold it up higher.
In it poke holes, on it draw moles in bowls.
Wet it, pet it, let it grow mold.
Punch it, scrunch it.
Paint it dark as a lark.
Use it as your bookmark.
Doodle hearts on it.
Make it a target, throw darts at it.
Do a test on it, write your best on it.
Plant it in the garden, let it harden.
Turn it into a plane, nah too lame.
Stuff it down a drain.
Erase all the lines, on it pour Heinz.
Put it in a book, let nobody look.
Fold it in half, feed it to a calf.
Send it, end it.
Hand it in as your term paper.

Complex Haiku Amusing Musing

Currently marked safe
from a relationship with
Muse. Complicated.

a note from the author

I've heard hundreds of times: "Words are important." Words communicate and crystalize thoughts, can paint a picture and teach values. Words matter. Word meanings matter. Define your terms. Though meanings may change over time, evoking different conclusions by different people depending on experience, they can also easily be distorted for innocuous or nefarious purposes.

My husband seemed surprised when I mentioned I loved the song "Wild Horses" by the Stones. He associated it with heroin addiction because he heard it when it was first out and in those days acquaintances were OD'ing in droves. My interpretation was that it was a little ditty about God's undying love for each of us and our eternal souls. Of course, I know the song is about what the writers say it is. Amazing how experiences affect the way those lyrics landed on us. Changes happen when words are captured and then are released or escape into the wild. We're all looking at the same thing: interpreting.

Poetry has always been for me a bit of a brain break before my brain brakes or breaks. I happily spit out words all over a piece of paper, then play with them and puzzle them out as one way to process emotions, thoughts, and ideas. One big motivator for me to take pen to paper is anger, so some of what you'll find in my poetry pages reflects that. This small compilation of musings on a life, during a life, covering the most sublime and aggravating experiences is my mosaic.

I don't write steadily. The majority of these poems were written before the year 2000, with some as early as the 1970s. Whenever the muse inspires and motivates, I play. I play with words: word sounds, syllables, rhymes, pauses, and meanings. It's relaxing fun for me and I hope you enjoy the result.

Throwing these poems out into the world feels a bit like a "little drummer boy" moment. Pa-rum pum pum pum. I have no gift to bring, but this little gift of me working my pen. All for you.

"I want to read some unknown poems
written by some unkown poet!"
~ said no one ever

Maybe just buy some
Bubble Gum at the Register.